BIRMINGHAM
IN THE
SIXTIES

VOL 1

Alton & Jo Douglas

Back of Geach Street, off Summer Lane, 5th December 1966.

© 1998 Alton and Jo Douglas
ISBN 1 85858 118 4
Published by Brewin Books Ltd., Doric House, 56 Alcester Road, Studley, Warwickshire B80 7LG.
Printed by Warwick Printing Co. Ltd., Caswell Road, Leamington Spa, Warwickshire CV31 1QD.
Layout by Alton and Jo Douglas
7th Impression May 2005

Masshouse Lane/Redditch Road, Kings Norton, 11th October 1967.

Front Cover: Snow Hill/Steelhouse Lane, 28th June 1961.

Contents

BREWIN BOOKS LTD

Doric House, 56 Alcester Road,
Studley, Warwickshire B80 7LG

Tel: 01527 854228 Fax: 01527 852746

Vat Registration No. 705 0077 73

Dear Nostalgic,

Well, it's your fault! As soon as "Birmingham in the Fifties" came out, copies were snapped up (it went into reprint within a month) and everyone said that the next subject had to be the sixties – so here it is.

It's easy to dismiss the decade as a period of great liberalism, inspired by an imagined new-found freedom, that would create so much havoc in the years to come; a decade that inspired such phrases as "If you can remember it, you weren't part of it", or John Lennon's "Nothing happened in the sixties except that we all dressed up" – a time when Vivian Stanshall and the Bonzo Dog Doo-Dah Band coined "Cool Britannia", which is still with us today. However, it was far more than just that. Youth seemed to come into its own for the first time, with hair longer, skirts shorter and the Beatles changing popular music forever. In Birmingham it was an era of re-building (although not to everyone's liking) but, despite the impression that everything was changing, there was still a great deal of traditionalism around. How often Royal visitors came to town and how we turned out in our thousands to greet them! Our magnificent Town Hall seemed to be in constant use. We still went to the pictures and the theatre and to sporting occasions. We worked hard and we played hard, as Brummies have throughout the ages.

All of this, and more, is reflected in our book – along with lots and lots of those street scenes that we know mean so much to you.

Yours, in friendship,

Park Garage Autos (B'ham) Ltd., Warwards Lane, Selly Oak, 31st May 1965.

1960

Brookvale Road, Witton, 1960.

Burlington Passage, off Lower Temple Street, 6th January 1960.

Edwards Road, with Orphanage Road in view, Erdington, c 1960.

Kyotts Lake Road, Sparkbrook, 10th February 1960.

Stechford Lane, with Stechford Road on the right, Ward End, 23rd February 1960.

Great Lister Street, Nechells Green, 1960.

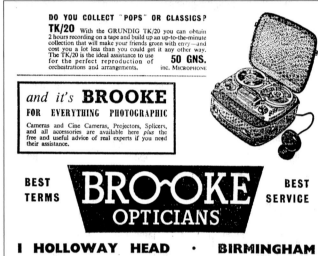

St Lukes Road/Hanover Street, Highgate, March 1960.

High Street, Aston, 1960.

Minister of Transport, Rt Hon Ernest Marples, MP, cuts the tape to open the first section of the Inner Ring Road, 11th March 1960. Accompanying him is the Lord Mayor, Alderman J.H. Lewis and Councillor D.S. Thomas, Chairman of the Public Works Committee.

Edgbaston High School, Hagley Road, 1960.

Kings Norton Grammar School Cross Country Team, c 1960.

The Lord Mayor and Lady Mayoress, Alderman and Mrs J.H. Lewis, watch as their sons, Richard and Roger, help to operate telephone machines, during a tour of the Birmingham Mail premises, 8th April 1960.

IN ALL its years of history and pageantry, Westminster Abbey had never known a Royal wedding quite like it.

The Queen's sister was marrying an untitled commoner — a plain Mister.

The marriage of Princess Margaret to Mr. Antony Armstrong-Jones on May 6, was the Royal occasion of the year.

It was the first wedding for which television cameras were installed in Westminster Abbey and as a result an estimated 300,000,000 saw the ceremony.

All over the country, Britain stood still as workers downed tools to see the Royal wedding on television.

Six hairdressing salons in Birmingham installed TV sets specially to allow their customers to watch the ceremony.

The wedding of Princess Margaret caught the imagination of millions overseas, as television and radio took Westminster Abbey into homes and cafés round the world.

Europeans crowded round television sets to watch the live Eurovision broadcast of the ceremony, which was clearly received almost everywhere.

Americans had their first glimpse of the Princess over the breakfast coffee and rolls, and jet aircraft took off from British and French airfields with longer films of the wedding to be shown over North American networks later in the day.

To some parts of the world the wedding came during the night, but many people in New Zealand, Hongkong, Malaya, and America sacrificed hours of sleep to hear the shortwave radio broadcast from London.

Some British forces overseas were given time off and many soldiers in Germany watched the Eurovision broadcast in homes or on sets in their barracks.

Princess Margaret, accompanied by her brother-in-law, the Duke of Edinburgh, on her way to Westminster Abbey.

Watching the Royal Wedding, Midlands Electricity Board Showroom, Dale End.

City of Birmingham Day Nurseries, Farm Street, Hockley, May 1960.

THE OBJECTS OF THE MOTHERS' UNION.

1. To uphold the Sanctity of Marriage.

In the words "to uphold the Sanctity of Marriage," the Mothers' Union affirms the Christian principle of the permanence of the relationship between husband and wife.

2. To awaken in all Mothers a sense of their great responsibility in the training of their boys and girls—the Fathers and Mothers of the Future.

3. To organize in every place a band of Mothers who will unite in prayer and seek by their own example to lead their families in purity and holiness of life.

QUALIFICATIONS FOR MEMBERSHIP.

Membership is open to married women :

1. Who have been baptized, affirm their belief in the principle of infant baptism, and undertake to bring their children (if any) to Holy Baptism.

2. Who accept the teaching contained in the Apostles' Creed.

3. Who are faithful to their marriage vows.

4. Who declare their adherence to the three Central Objects.

PREPARATION.

" That there shall be a period of preparation of not less than three months before admission to the Mothers' Union.

Any exception to this rule must be sanctioned by the Central President, or by the President of a Federated Council, or by the General President for Ireland.

It is intended that preparation should include personal instruction by the Enrolling Member of each prospective Member." *Regulation No. 3.*

Branch :

St Stephens Selly Hill Church Hall

Time and Place of Meetings :

2.30 First Thursday of Each Month

Enrolling Member :

L. Cartwright

The Market Hall, seen from Lord Nelson's statue,
Bull Ring, 1960.

Stratford Road, Sparkhill, 1960.

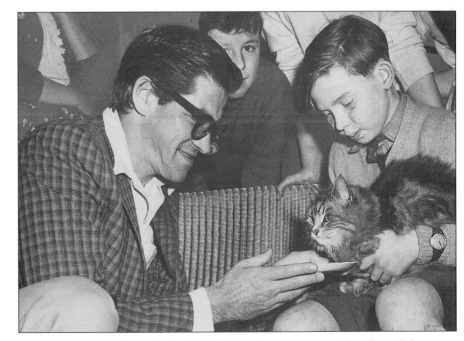

Popular vocalist, Michael Holliday, gives a saucer of milk to Tyloo,
winner of the pets' competition, at the ABC Cinema, Bristol Road,
21st May 1960. The cat's owner, Daniel Wragg, of Charlotte Road,
Edgbaston, won a visit to Belle Vue Zoo.

11

Canon Bryan Green preaching on the evils of apartheid in South Africa, St Martin's Church,
Spiceal Street, 31st May 1960.

Bull Street, 2nd August 1960. "No Parking" signs had just been erected, for the first time,
to keep the traffic moving.

Pershore Road, Cotteridge, 27th September 1960.

Summer Row, 30th September 1960.

Kings Hall Market, photographed from Lewis's and showing Lower Priory on the right, Old Square, September 1960.

Hockley Brook improvement under way, November 1960.

Demolition workers busy themselves, Corporation Street, November 1960.

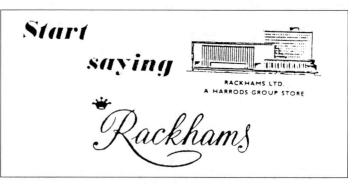
The final part of Rackhams was opened in November 1960.

Old Oscott Lane, with Dyas Road on the right, Great Barr, 16th December 1960.

High Street, Saltley, 1960.

Winson Green Road, December 1960.

The Alan Stokes Group help to celebrate New Year's Eve, somewhere in the city, 1960. The streamers in front of the drums give the clue as to the occasion.

Fisher & Ludlow Ltd., Kingsbury Road, Erdington, 1961.

Oxford Street, Digbeth, 1961.

Nelson Street, with Barker Street on the left,
Ladywood, February 1961.

Belchers Lane, Alum Rock, February 1961.

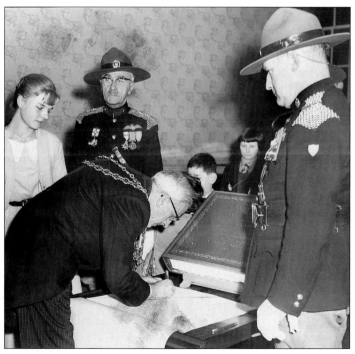

Flanked by members of the Legion of Frontiersmen,
the Lord Mayor, Alderman G.B. Boughton, signs the
"Book of Silence", Art Gallery, 7th February 1961.
It was part of an effort to provide schools for the
deaf in the Commonwealth.

Alum Rock Road, with Clodeshall Road on the left, February 1961.

Ansells Aston League darts' winners from the White Hart, Aston Road, 1961.

Warwick Road, Greet, 22nd February 1961.

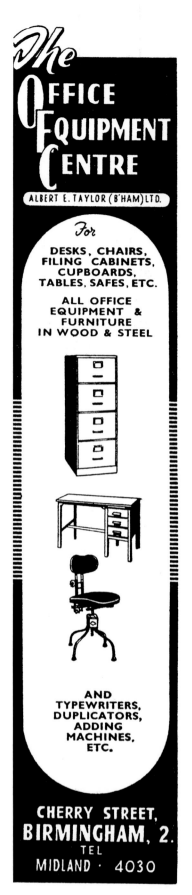

Local MP, Leonard Cleaver (centre) looks on as Mr H.J. Swinburne (left) Deputy Manager of the Yardley Ministry of Pensions' office, explains the new graduated pension scheme to Arthur Newey, 13th March 1961.

Phil King and the Couriers, Sheldon, 1961.

North Western Arcade, March 1961.

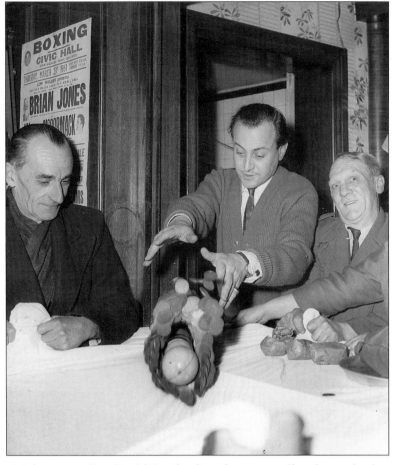

BIRMINGHAM SCHOOL OF MUSIC

SONATA RECITAL

HANNAH JONES
(Violin)

LILIAN NIBLETTE
(Piano)

in the

**CONCERT ROOM, BIRMINGHAM
AND MIDLAND INSTITUTE**
(Licensee E. A. Knight)

on

FRIDAY, 24th MARCH, 1961
at 7-30 p.m.

PROGRAMME THREEPENCE

BBC personality, David Jacobs, knocks over a pile of pennies in aid of spastic children, Witton Arms, Aston, 23rd March 1961.

Denis Howell, Labour candidate in the Small Heath by-election, tries out his loud-hailer at the back of his Coventry Road committee rooms, March 1961. He was successful in securing the seat.

Work starting on the underpass, Birchfield Road, Perry Barr, 3rd May 1961.

The helicopter carrying the Duke of Edinburgh arrives outside Baskerville House, 1st June 1961. He was here to open the Careers' Exhibition at Bingley Hall.

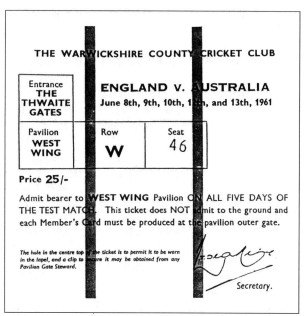

THE WARWICKSHIRE COUNTY CRICKET CLUB

| Entrance THE THWAITE GATES | ENGLAND v. AUSTRALIA June 8th, 9th, 10th, 12th, and 13th, 1961 | | |
| Pavilion WEST WING | Row W | Seat 46 |

Price 25/-

Admit bearer to WEST WING Pavilion ON ALL FIVE DAYS OF THE TEST MATCH. This ticket does NOT admit to the ground and each Member's Card must be produced at the pavilion outer gate.

The hole in the centre top of the ticket is to permit it to be worn in the lapel, and a clip to secure it may be obtained from any Pavilion Gate Steward.

Secretary.

Ken Wiggins services a Daimler limousine, Birmingham Co-operative Society Garages, Great Brook Street, Vauxhall, c 1961.

Dave Carpenter proudly shows off a brand-new D9 Midland Red bus, awaiting delivery, Carlyle Works, Edgbaston, 1961.

Aston Villa FC, League Cup winners, 1960/61.

TOWN HALL, BIRMINGHAM

TUESDAY 14th MARCH 1961
at 7 p.m.

THE CITY OF BIRMINGHAM CHOIR

WITH

THE CITY OF BIRMINGHAM SYMPHONY ORCHESTRA
Leader : MEYER STOLOW

REQUIEM (MOZART)

★

SYMPHONY of PSALMS (STRAWINSKY)

The junction of Oak Tree Lane and Bristol Road, Selly Oak, 1961.

Steelhouse Lane, 27th June 1961.

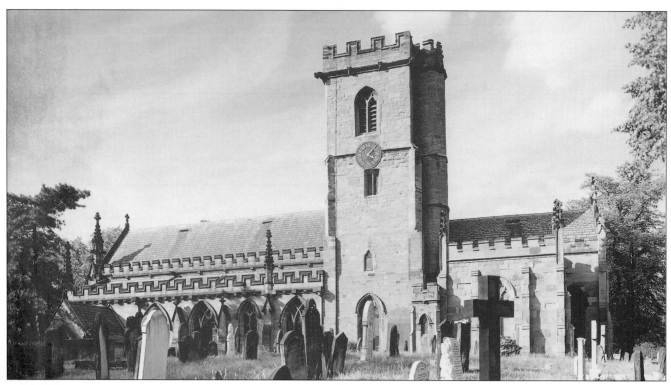

St Mary's Church, Hunters Road, Handsworth, September 1961.

Our own David Hughes pops a cork to celebrate the birth of his daughter. Gosta Green TV studios, 11th September 1961. The singer, who was appearing in "September Song", is seen with fellow artists Joyce Blackham and Rosemary Squires, under the watchful eye of producer, Philip Lewis.

The Everglades, Allen's Cross Working Men's Club, Merritts Brook Lane, Northfield, 1961.

The Des Anthony Trio, Highfield Club, Park Road, Moseley, 1961.

John Bright Street, with Suffolk Place on the right, 1961.

High Street, Erdington, 1961.

The foundations for the Rotunda are under way, 25th October 1961.

Birmingham Reference Library, Ratcliffe Place, 22nd November 1961.

Church Road, from Aldridge Road, Perry Barr, 1961.

IT would be interesting to know just how much the Dave Brubeck Quartet's current hit parade success was responsible for the two well-filled houses at Birmingham Town Hall last night.

Brubeck's heavy, relentless attacks on the keyboard contrasted with the lilting lyricism of Altoist Paul Desmond whose purity of tone must be unrivalled in the field of modern jazz.

Nimble Joe Morello even managed to make a marathon drum solo musically interesting and combined with basist Eugene Wright to give Brubeck and Desmond solid but unobtrusive support.

Dave Brubeck had a hit with his version of "Take Five". Town Hall, 23rd November 1961.

Lodge Road, Hockley, 13th December 1961.

27

Albert Walk, Harborne, 3rd January 1962.

Birchfield Road, with Mansfield Road just out of sight on the right, 15th January 1962.

The entrance to Kings Heath Station, High Street, 1962.

Berkeley Road East, Hay Mills, 1st March 1962.

Shaftsmoor Lane, Acocks Green, March 1962.

Cuckoo Road, Nechells, 15th March 1962. Note the wartime Anderson shelter and the mangle – and doesn't that loaf look mouth-watering!

Frank Ifield teaches pupils to sing his hit number, "I Remember You", at his old school, Springfield School, College Road, Moseley, 1962.

Burlington Street Secondary Modern School for Girls, Aston, 1962.

30

Hill Street, with Hinckley Street on the left, 1962.

Comedian, Arthur Haynes, signs an autograph for David Green, Tudor Bingo Club, Kings Heath, 28th March 1962.

The Lord Mayor, Alderman E.E. Mole (right), receives a camel saddle from Arab representatives, 28th March 1962.

Mike Sheridan and the Nightriders, 1962. The group is still operating, out of the city, to this day.

32

The old and the new Woolworth's buildings, Bull Ring, 12th September 1962.

Birchfield Road, Perry Barr, 1962.

American singer, Chubby Checker, joined on stage by some of the audience, Town Hall, 20th September 1962.

The opening of the new Littlewoods' store by the Lord and Lady Mayoress, Alderman and Mrs E.W. Horton, High Street, 20th September 1962.

– and the crowds wait for goods on offer.

34

Woodbridge Road, Moseley, 21st September 1962.

Stechford Road, Stechford, 21st September 1962.

An important chore of the day – checking the menu,
Austin works, Longbridge, November 1962.

The Blessing and Opening Ceremony at the Polish
Catholic Centre, Bordesley Street, 8th November 1962.
The Deputy Lord Mayor, Alderman E. E. Mole,
performed the honours.

Broad Street, with Easy Row on the left, 1962.

Holloway Circus, with the traffic negotiating the new island, Horse Fair is to the left, November 1962.

Festival of Remembrance service, conducted by the Rt Rev George Sinker, Town Hall, 11th November 1962.

1963

THE LAMBERT COURT HOTEL
AND
LICENSED RESTAURANT
336, HAGLEY ROAD
EDGBASTON 17

Stands in 1½ acres of picturesque gardens, so rare in the hustle and bustle of this large city • Throughout The Lambert Court there is an atmosphere of friendliness and efficiency • Here you will find excellent cuisine (featured in the "Good Food Guide") and Wines to suit all tastes. Restaurant open until 11 p.m.

Available for
FUNCTIONS • PRIVATE DINNER DANCES
WEDDINGS & ANNIVERSARIES

Parking for 50 Cars.
PHONE BEA 2201-2.

ARNOLD'S STORES LTD.
FAMILY GROCERS

PROVISION, FRUIT AND WINE MERCHANTS AND ITALIAN WAREHOUSEMEN

Established over 60 years and still famous for
QUALITY and SERVICE

THE "EDGBASTON" GROCERS

ALL OUR GROCERIES AND PROVISIONS ARE CAREFULLY SELECTED FROM THE FINEST SOURCES OF SUPPLY

May we deliver to you?

Head Office
210-211 MONUMENT ROAD
EDGBASTON   Phone: EDG 3564/5

And at
355 HAGLEY ROAD, EDGBASTON
197½ HAGLEY ROAD, EDGBASTON
MERE GREEN, FOUR OAKS

Best sellers in Birmingham

FICTION
Alistair MacLean: "Ice Station Zebra."
Dennis Wheatley: "The Sultan's Daughter."
D. E. Stevenson: "The Blue Sapphire."
Morris West: "The Shoes of the Fisherman."
Sergeanne Golon: "Angelique in Love."

NON-FICTION
John A. T. Robinson: "Honest to God."
Egon Ronay: "Guide to 1,000 Eating Places."
Peter Roberts: "Veteran and Vintage Cars."
James Baldwin: "The Fire Next Time."
O. Fielding Clarke: "For Christ's Sake."
Stirling Moss: "All But My Life."
Bryan Morgan (Ed.): "The Railway-Lover's Companion."

Garden House Hotel
154/160, HAGLEY ROAD (A456) EDGBASTON

The Hagley Suite
(Banqueting Accommodation 150)

STUDIO BAR FULLY LICENSED
STEAK BAR   SANDWICH BAR
NOW OPEN

RESTAURANT OPEN OCT. 14th

HAGLEY SUITE NOW AVAILABLE

CHRISTMAS RESERVATIONS NOW ACCEPTED

Car Parking facilities for 150 cars

For full details either write or telephone the Manager
Edgbaston 5212 & 4591

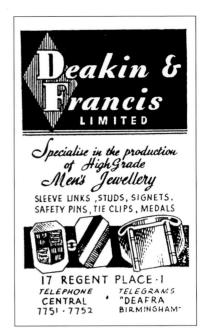
The Rotunda grows before our eyes, February 1963. This unusual angle
is taken from the Inner Ring Road.

Rogers Road/Washwood Heath Road, Ward End, 1963.

Balden Road/Hampton Court Road, Harborne, 1963.

Easy Row, with Edmund Street on the right, 1963.

Paradise Street, at the junction with Easy Row on the left, 1963.

Abbey Street, Hockley, 1963.

Ludgate Hill/Great Charles Street, 1963.

Washwood Heath Road, Ward End, 1963.

Traffic problems developing at the junction of Ravenhurst Street/Camp Hill, 2nd May 1963.

League Cup glory for Birmingham City FC, 1963.

Aston Boys FC, 1963.

Part of the Brum Beat, Denny Laine and the
Diplomats, 1963.

Highfield Road, Hall Green, 1963.

Warwick Road/Mountford Street, Greet, 1963.

The Queen tours the Bull Ring market as part of her visit to see the reconstruction taking place in the area, 24th May 1963. Accompanying her is Councillor Mrs N. Smith, Chairman of the Markets and Fairs Committee.

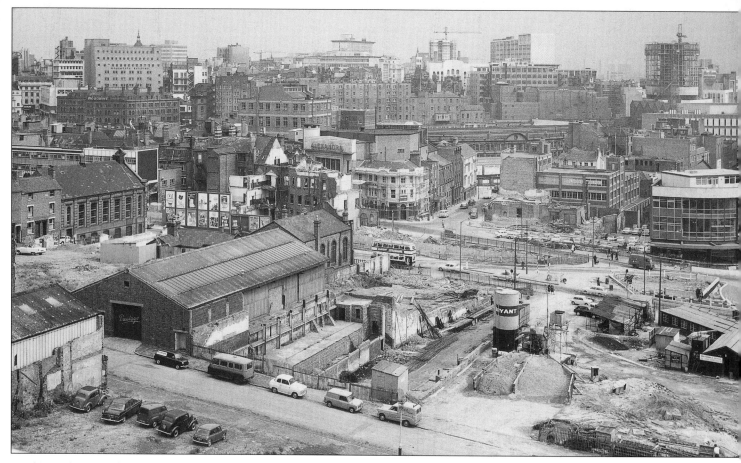

A good example of development in the city taking place, with the Alexandra Theatre (left of centre) pinpointing the position of John Bright Street, 19th July 1963.

*Grandiose plans for a multi-million-pound new look for Birmingham's New Street Station came out in May.

People of the future, we were told, would not recognise the place. That could be true.

Because in May of 1963 Birmingham was told the new building would give the city the first combined entertainments centre and railway station in the country.

It was to include two cinemas, a restaurant, bowling centre, shopping precinct and car parks.

The scheme was timed to be completed by 1967 when the electrification of the Manchester - Liverpool - Birmingham - Euston line was hoped to be finished.

Elkington Street Infants' School, Aston, 1963.

The Great Train Robbery.

First reports, on the morning of August 8, were breath-taking enough.

In a Jesse James-style raid a gang successfully ambushed the Glasgow-London mail train. At the time there was talk of £200,000.

Within the next 24 hours the figure was to grow dramatically as though inflation had just been invented. There was a suggestion that the final figure might even top the £3 million mark.

But by the end of August 9 Scotland Yard at least had the cash situation sorted out. The money missing amounted to a whopping £2,626,000 in used bank notes.

Surrounded by some of her younger constituents Edith Pitt, MP, signs autographs for boys of Hallfield School, Edgbaston. House of Commons, 1st August 1963.

TOMORROW is Friday the 13th of September, and only three brave couples are going to be married at Birmingham Register Office, where September has been a most popular month for weddings. Last Saturday 78 couples faced the registrars.

Though Birmingham people are normally much too hard-headed to bother about such superstitions, there is something about the double, if silly, menace of Friday the Thirteenth which deters the hardiest from travelling, taking driving tests, making important decisions and visiting the dentist.

It will probably be the same in December when there is another Friday the thirteenth this year.

Senior staff meeting at Woolworth's, Bull Ring, 25th September 1963. The third floor had finally opened, a year after the first part of the building was in operation.

Still the Rotunda grows, 1963.

Holyhead Road, Handsworth, October 1963.

President Kennedy, who was
assassinated on 22nd November 1963.

BIRMINGHAM council house rents are to go up by an average of 10s. a week on pre-war houses and 5s. a week on post-war homes.

HOW THE INCREASES VARY

Type	PRE-WAR Present Net	New Net	Inc.	POST-WAR Present Net	New Net	Inc.
Bungalow, 1 bed.	10/7	18/-	7/5	15/5	27/-	11/7
Flat, 1 bed.	10/7	18/8	8/1	21/11	23/3	1/4
Flat, 2 bed.	18/4	24/-	5/8	31/7	32/3	8
Flat, 3 bed.	20/5	27/5	7/-	31/3	33/-	1/9
Maisonette, 2 bed.	—	—		25/10	34/2	8/4
Maisonette, 3 bed.	—			32/1	36/-	3/11
House, 2 bed.	18/7	28/2	9/7	29/11	35/8	5/9
House, 3 bed.	22/-	32/8	10/8	33/5	38/8	5/3

The new rents have been calculated on the basis of 0.9 times the gross value of the dwelling. Old people will have a special rebate which will mean they will not be affected.

The rent increases will be introduced in 5s. stages from December. Old people will be exempt from paying more.

The rate fund subsidy on normal municipal housing is to be dropped completely, giving a possible saving of more than £2,000,000 over the next five years.

The subsidy on ordinary council houses is £786,000 a year at present.

Under the new scheme, ratepayers will bear the cost of rent rebates to needy tenants

Highbrook Service Station, Highgate Road, Sparkbrook, 1963.

Rehearsal time for the Ron Astell Big Band, Hungry Man Restaurant,
Broad Street, 1963.

A B Row/Howe Street, 12th December 1963.

Harborne Lane, Selly Oak, 6th February 1964.

Stars of the Alexandra Theatre's pantomime, "Babes in the Wood", rural comic Billy Burden and singer Ronnie Carroll, try their hand at ten-pin bowling, Pavilion Bowl, Wylde Green, 8th February 1964.

Local-girl-made-good, Susan Maughan, appears on ABC TV's "Thank Your Lucky Stars", 8th February 1964. She was there to sing her version of "Hey Lover". Previously, she had been the resident singer with the Sonny Rose Orchestra, at the West End Ballroom.

St Catherine of Siena Roman Catholic Church, Bristol Street, 14th February 1964.

In order to publicise the British Empire Cancer Campaign's Spring Fair, at the Town Hall, the Lord Mayor and Lady Mayoress, Alderman Dr Louis Glass and Mrs Glass, drive in a model T Ford (known as a "Tin Lizzie"), Colmore Row, 12th March 1964. With them is the Chairman of the Organising Committee, Mr S.V. Mercer.

Great Colmore Street, Edgbaston, 1964.

Sampson Road/Henley Street, Sparkbrook, 20th May 1964.

Sydenham Road/Golden Hillock Road, Small Heath,
22nd May 1964.

NEW features announced for the Hillman Minx de luxe last week are also in the Singer Gazelle for 1964, the Rootes Group said today.

A new roof line, re-styled rear window and rear wings are accompanied by wider rear doors.

Front wheel disc brakes are fitted, suspension and steering are improved and all greasing points are eliminated with a lengthening of the intervals between servicing to 3,000 miles.

Individual front seats replace the previous bench seating and a redesigned dashboard, finished in polished walnut veneer, is fitted.

The car costs £723 (including £125 purchase tax) which is £16 more than the current model now superseded. Borg Warner automatic transmission is available as an extra at £90 (including £15 purchase tax).

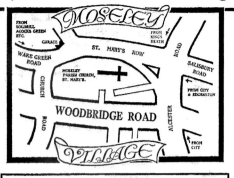

The Regimental Band of the Royal Warwickshire Fusiliers play alongside the diesel locomotive named after the regiment, Platform 7, Snow Hill Station, 22nd May 1964.

The Duke of Edinburgh looks over his shoulder to acknowledge the crowds during his visit to open the new Bull Ring Centre, 29th May 1964.

MEN'S double-fronted shirts - with three collars cost 18s. 9d., tufted broadloom carpet was 12s. 11d. a square yard, and pure silk stockings 5s. 11d. a pair.

There were good bargains to be had at the 1964 January sales.

At the "expensive" end of the trade, the fashion-conscious woman could buy a winter coat reduced from 25 guineas to £18. And a man could look discreetly smart in a suit reduced from 32 guineas to £25.

Junior 2, Elkington Street Primary School, Aston, May 1964.

This was the year that brought in the Mini-skirt, and saw the Midlands take a key role in television entertainment and debate.

Mrs. Mary Whitehouse launched her Clean-Up TV Campaign in Birmingham: "Swizzlewick" proved a doomed TV excursion into council chambers of local government — and a series called "Crossroads" made a tentative entrance.

Elmbridge Road, Kingstanding, 9th June 1964.

Great Hampton Street, Hockley, 1964.

The Lord Mayor, Alderman Frank Price, leads young cyclists along the
experimental cycle park, Aston, 29th July 1964.

Tony Britton stands on the roof of the Market Hotel, overlooking New Street Station, 20th September 1964. He was appearing at the Hippodrome and had been asked to pose in that particular spot because his father had once been the hotel's landlord.

Bristol Road South, Northfield, September 1964.

Green Lane, Small Heath, 26th October 1964.

ONE person who will remember the Bristol-road South water mains bursts for a long time is 12-years-old Michael Massingham, of 173, Black Haynes-road. On Monday, while cycling in the area, he fell into the water-filled crater which has been created by the bursts and clung to the crumbling side before being pulled out by Pol.-Cons. F. Wigley.

Michael's cycle was still missing somewhere in the crater on Wednesday and a spokesman for the Water Department told me it was either buried under the mud or had got into one of the pipes.

Bilton Grange Road, Yardley, October 1964

High Park Corner/Nechells Park Road, Nechells Green; 2nd November 1964.

New Town Row, Aston, 1964.

Bloomsbury Institution, Fowler Street,
Nechells, 3rd November 1964.

Slade Road, Erdington, 1964.

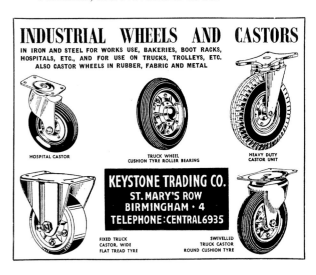

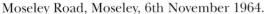

Moseley Road, Moseley, 6th November 1964.

Watford Road, Cotteridge, 10th November 1964.

The new underpass takes shape, Hagley Road West, Quinton, 12th November 1964.

Newbridge Road/Hobmoor Road, Small Heath, 16th November 1964.

Toy Fair, Lewis's, 12th December 1964.

Holt Street, Aston, 1965.

Sir Winston Churchill, who passed away on
the 24th January 1965.

Part of a childrens' play area, Newgate Street,
Nechells Green, 4th March 1965.

Pershore Road, between Hazelwell Road and Ivy Road, Stirchley, 25th March 1965.

The Beatles at a recording of "Thank Your Lucky Stars", ATV, Alpha Television Studios,
Aston, 28th March 1965.

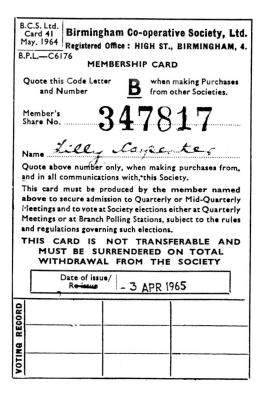

The Lady Mayoress, Mrs Frank Price, receives a donation of £10
towards the Lord Mayor's Appeal for Mentally Handicapped
Children, collected by members of the 116th B'ham St Andrews'
Brownie Pack, of Handsworth. Mayor's Parlour, 12th April 1965.

The most famous hairdresser in the country , TV personality,
Raymond "Mr Teazie Weazie", after crowning the Tulip Queen,
20th April 1965.

ONE of the finest urban road systems in Europe. This will be Birmingham's £27,000,000 Inner Ring Road when it is completed five years from now.

The three-mile Ring Road, mainspring for all the city centre rebuilding, is now more than half completed, in terms of acquisition of property and clearance, if not in actual road construction.

Sections from Holloway Circus to Carrs Lane and from Colmore Circus to St. Chad's Circus have been completed.

Holloway Circus itself, with the underpass running beneath from Bristol Street to Suffolk Street, will be ready for the spring. The outward bound carriageway of the underpass is being opened on December 6.

Bristol Road, with Wellington Road on the right, Edgbaston,
April 1965.

First day of the summer sale, in the lingerie department,
Lewis's, 29th June 1965.

Lancaster Place, 29th June 1965.

Albert Street, running up to High Street, City Centre, 3rd August 1965.

Bull Ring and St Martin's,
Summer 1965.

Still more demolition, in the name of progress,
Stephenson Place, looking up Corporation Street,
3rd September 1965.

Personal radios, for Police use, take the place of the old kerbside emergency telephones, Old Square, 1965.

Carl Wayne and the Vikings, c 1965.

Lonsdale Road, Harborne, 7th September 1965.

Baldwins Lane/Gracemere Crescent, Hall Green,
September 1965.

Monument Road, Ladywood, 15th September 1965.

Coleys Lane, Northfield, 8th October 1965.

Bob Martin is helped by the staff of Dunlop's service
department to celebrate his retirement, after 50 years
with the company, Fort Dunlop, Erdington,
c 1965.

After performing the opening ceremony at the new Post and Mail
buildings, Princess Margaret, along with Chairman, Sir Eric
Clayson, greets the waiting crowds, Colmore Circus, 26th October
1965. Lord Snowdon can be seen, at the rear, also acknowledging
the enthusiastic reception.

Birmingham Gun-Barrel Proof House
(for Small Arms), Banbury Street, October 1965

Residents of Granville Street (off Broad Street) after a campaign to
get them re-housed has proved to be successful, October 1965.

Wheeler Street/Bridge Street West, Newtown, 5th November 1965.

Beeches Road, just before Hassop Road, Great Barr, 5th November 1965.

Colmore Circus, 7th November 1965. The Gaumont Cinema, on the left, was showing the long-running film, "The Sound of Music".

Great Russell Street, Newtown, 8th November 1965.

Tealby Grove/ Milner Road, Selly Oak, 7th December 1965.

Ward Street, Aston, 1965.

Woolworth's Christmas Party, Bull Ring, c 1965.

1966

County Headquarters,
Birmingham.
January, 1966.

Dear Wolf Cub,

1966 is Wolf Cub Golden Jubilee Year. Yes, you are fifty years old—at least not you, but Cub Scouting has its 50th birthday this year!

A very happy birthday to each Wolf Cub in Birmingham Scout County, and if I were to say this separately to each one of you, I should have to say it over five thousand times.

How many Cubs are there in your Pack? If you turn to the back page you will read a Special Challenge that the Chief Scout has sent to you.

All the Cubs in the United Kingdom—and that is nearly 240,000 Cubs—will celebrate this Golden Jubilee.

Through the "Jubilee Birthday Card Scheme" we hope to link the Cubs in the U.K. with the other half million Cubs in the Commonwealth, all of whom have the same Chief Scout—Sir Charles Maclean. We are delighted that he will be in Birmingham on February 25th and 26th, so some of you will be seeing him, and what a wonderful welcome he will have!

There are over three million Cubs in the world who will be linked this year by the Birthday Card Scheme. You are indeed a member of a World Wide Brotherhood.

So, a very happy Birthday Year to you—and make the most of your go'den opportunities this year and in the future.

Good wishes,

EVELYN H. SLARKE,
(A.C.C. Cubs).

CUB EVENTS IN 1966

Your own Cubmaster will tell you about these, and other events that will take place during the year

January: Jubilee Birthday Cards. Scrapbooks.

February: B.P. Special Pack Meeting.

February 25th (Friday): 7 p.m., CUB CONCERT in Birmingham Town Hall. To be attended by the Chief Scout.

April: Special Easter Good Turns.

May 14th (Saturday): CUB OPEN DAY at Yorks Wood, Birmingham.

June 4th: Special National Pack Meeting. "FIFTY YEARS' JUBILEE CELEBRATION." A broadcast message by the Chief Scout.

June 25th (Saturday): "ADVENTURE UNKNOWN." Musical Pageant Play in the Royal Albert Hall, London, by London Cubs.

July 2nd: CUB AND SCOUT RALLY at Handsworth Park. A Jubilee Pageant presented by Wolf Cubs. A member of the Royal Family will attend.

July, August, September, October: CUB NATIONAL "GOOD TURN". Collection of Silver Paper for the Guide Dogs for the Blind Association.

September — October: "Keep Britain Tidy Campaign."

October 30th: 3 p.m., THANKSGIVING SERVICE FOR CUBS in Birmingham Town Hall.

December: Each Pack is asked to provide two Birthday Cakes—one to eat at their Pack Meeting first week in December—and the other to give away.

FUTURE YEARS — BECOME A SCOUT — and further opportunities will be available for you!

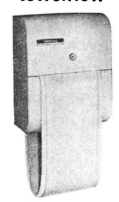

The Birmingham-formed Spencer Davis Group top the charts with "Keep on Running", January 1966.

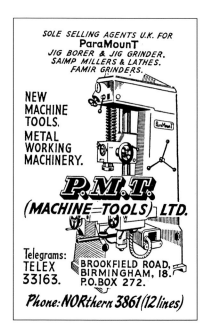

Arthur Horrage commemorates his 90th birthday with a game of snooker, Ward End Sons of Rest, Ward End Park, Washwood Heath Road, 26th February 1966.

Two characters from the BBC Light Programme, "The Archers", Hilary Newcombe ("Polly") and Alan Devereux ("Sid Perks") relax in Cannon Hill Park, 13th March 1966.

Broad Street, 1966.

The Lord and Lady Mayoress, Alderman and Mrs George Corbyn Barrow, look at some of the shoes distributed by the Birmingham Mail Christmas Tree Fund, with the Chairman of the Central Committee, Alderman Sir Joseph Balmer, at the fund's depot, Crawford Street, Saltley, 11th March 1966.

Pershore Road/Dell Road, Kings Norton, 25th March 1966.

Rowheath Road/Midland Road, Cotteridge, 25th March 1966.

The swing to Labour in Birmingham was 6.7 per cent — one of the highest in the country. They polled more votes in the city than all other parties put together.

Labour regained Perry Barr, increased all their majorities, and sliced Tory majorities at Handsworth and Selly Oak to the bone.

THE MIDLANDS car industry received a body-blow from the harsh economic measures taken by the re-elected Labour Government in 1966.

The May 3 Budget, introduced by Jim Callaghan, had been basically "no change" — but the new Selective Employment Tax was destined to become highly unpopular.

● VILLA PARK was one of the grounds that played host to the World Cup soccer spectacular in the summer.

The World Cup Final brought England and West Germany together at Wembley.

The game was a cliffhanger. West Germany scored to make it 2-2 in the dying moments of the match. Two goals by Geoff Hurst gave England victory in extra time.

Constitution Hill Service Station, Howard Street/Constitution Hill, 1966.

Kingstanding Road, from the corner of Dyas Road, Perry Barr, 3rd June 1966.

Tyseley Hill Road, with Tyseley Station on the brow of the hill, June 1966.

Ninevah Road, Handsworth, 1966.

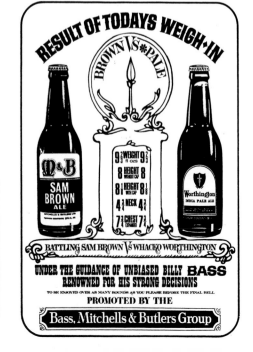

Prince Albert Street, Bordesley Green, 1966.

Waterloo Street/Colmore Row, 20th June 1966.

Aston University (top centre) Gosta Green, 24th July 1966.

Filming starts on "Privilege", starring Paul Jones and Jean Shrimpton, Pinfold Street, 29th August 1966.

Wheeler Street, Lozells, 1966.

Warwickshire CCC captain, Mike Smith, holds aloft the Gillette trophy, after defeating Worcestershire in the final at Lords, 3rd September 1966.

The Bordesley to Snow Hill viaduct, seen from Bordesley, with the city centre skyline in the background,
5th September 1966.

Stratford Road, Hall Green, 5th September 1966.

Kettlehouse Road, Kingstanding, 13th September 1966.

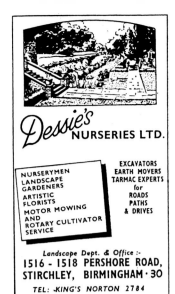

Keeley Street, Bordesley, 15th September 1966.

Wilton Street, Lozells, 19th September 1966.

Station Street, September 1966.

Hagley Road, from Five Ways, October 1966.

Beacon Motors Ltd., Aston Road, 1966.

Kyrwicks Lane, with Montpelier Street in view,
Sparkbrook, 1966.

Aston and Perry Barr Institute of Further Education
(Bloomsbury Centre) Goodrick Street, Nechells, 1966.

Lemon Tree, one of the many talented groups that were based in
Birmingham, 1966.

Berners Street, Lozells, 1966.

Lunch at the Over 60's Club for the Lord and Lady Mayoress, Alderman and Mrs Harold Tyler, Highgate Street, Balsall Heath, 15th October 1966.

Sprinting for bargains at the New Year Sale, Greys, Bull Street, 30th December 1966.

1967

Gooch Street, Highgate, 1967.

Richmond Road, Stechford, 1967.

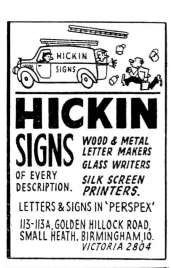

The West End Cinema, Suffolk Street, 24th February 1967. Less than a month later it closed.

Camden Street, Brookfields, 1967.

Ford Street/Lodge Road, Spring Hill, 3rd March 1967.

85

Booking clerk, Mr T. Jackson, on the last day of main-line services, Snow Hill Station, 4th March 1967.

Early morning commuters leave Snow Hill Station, 3rd March 1967.

Sir Stanley Raymond, Chairman of the British Railways Board, officially opens the new New Street Station, 6th March 1967.

Roy Orbison, the American singer with a succession of hits (including "Pretty Woman") sits astride a BSA motorcycle and meets his local fans, 9th March 1967.

Wyrley Hall FC display their trophies, after a season in which they had won the Youth Leader's Cup and the Britwell Coronation Shield. Witton, 1966/67.

Alec McCowen (centre) plays the title role in "Hadrian the Seventh" in its premiere performance, Birmingham Repertory Theatre, 8th May 1967.

Linden Road, Bournville, 10th July 1967.

Chester Road, Castle Bromwich, July 1967.

Albert Road, from Park Road, Aston, 1967.

Bull Ring, August 1967.

Shaun, the mascot of the Irish Guards, welcomes the Lord Mayor and Lady Mayoress, Alderman and Mrs James Meadows, at the opening of the Buy British exhibition at Rackhams, 8th August 1967.

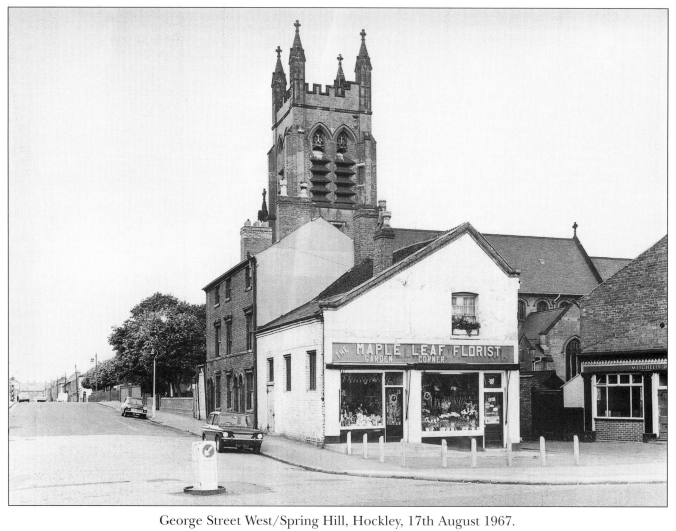

George Street West/Spring Hill, Hockley, 17th August 1967.

Suffolk Street, with Baskerville House at the top left, 4th September 1967.

Hagley Road, with Five Ways directly ahead, 1967.

Girls from the Miss Selfridge store-within-a-store,
show off the latest fashions, Lewis's,
10th September 1967.

A Roaring Twenties Ball proves to be an enormous success, as part of the city's Festival of Entertainments,
Town Hall, 21st September 1967.

Bristol Road, Selly Oak, 1967.

Our own pop group, The Move, display the latest styles,
prior to setting out on a UK tour, 5th October 1967.

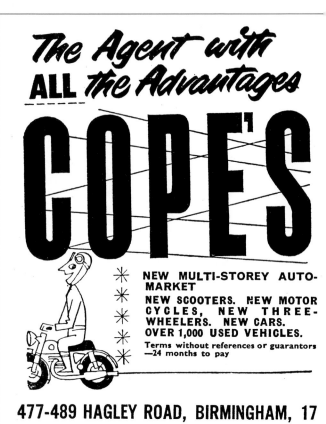

Gladman and Norman Ltd., Spencer Street,
Jewellery Quarter, 1967.

Wheeleys Road, from Carpenter Road, Edgbaston, 1967.

Central Square, Erdington, 1967.

ATV presenters, Rosemary Dunnage and Pat Astley, show boys of
the Training Ship Vernon Sea Cadet Unit how to shoot,
at the Unit's Trafalgar Dance, Tower Ballroom, Edgbaston,
31st October 1967.

Upper Cox Street/Balsall Heath
Road, Balsall Heath, 1967.

Lawrence Street/Duke Street, Aston, 1967.

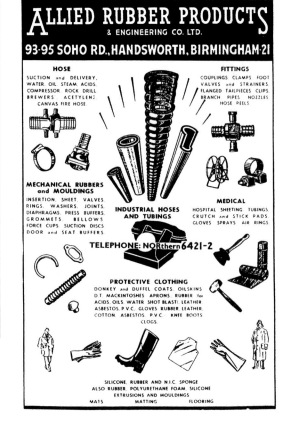

Blakesley Road/Stoney Lane, Yardley, 1967.

Hobmoor Road, Yardley, 15th December 1967.

A carol service was the attraction for the Lord Mayor and Lady Mayoress, Alderman and Mrs J.S. Meadows, Belgrave Junior School, Mary Street, Balsall Heath, 19th December 1967.

New Year's Eve revellers, Chamberlain Square, 1967.

1968

THE comprehensive education debate entered a new phase when the controlling Conservative group on Birmingham City Council introduced a compromise plan.

They proposed to replace the 11-plus examination with a system of "guided parental choice."

Twenty-five per cent of children would go to grammar schools, and the remainder to comprehensives.

Sherbourne Road/Longmore Street, Balsall Heath, January 1968.

Upper Thomas Street, Aston, 12th January 1968.

Ladypool Road, Balsall Heath, March 1968.

Wheeler Street, from Clifford Street, Lozells, March 1968.

Aston Hall Road, 1968.

Lennox Street/Clifford Street, Lozells, 4th March 1968.

Queens Hotel, Church Lane/Queens Road, Aston, 1968.

Sheepcote Street, Edgbaston, 1968.

Osler Street/Reservoir Road, Ladywood, 21st March 1968.

Coxwell Road/Hyde Road, with Clark Street ahead, Ladywood, 29th March 1968.

Hawthorn Road, Erdington, 30th April 1968.

The Delta Metal Co Apprentices' football team,
from Dartmouth Street, 1968.

City of Birmingham Civil Defence Corps
Disbandment Ceremony
Admit Mr. J. S. Kendall

Council Chamber, Council House   May 10th, 1968
Victoria Square   1930 hrs for 2000 hrs

BUCKINGHAM PALACE

On the occasion of the disbandment of the
Civil Defence Corps and the Auxiliary Fire Service,
I send to all members my appreciation and sincere
thanks for the loyal and devoted service they
have given to this country, some for many years and
some in wartime as well as peace.
This is a sad day for you; but your disbandment
in no way lessens the value of your services.
The spirit of comradeship you have shown,
and the example you have set in preparing yourselves
for the relief of human suffering and the welfare
of your fellow countrymen, have been an
inspiration and an encouragement to us all.

ELIZABETH R.

Spencer Street/Northampton Street, Hockley, 1968.

Kennedy Gardens, with St Chad's in the background, 1968.

The Lord Mayor, Alderman Charles Simpson, performs the ceremony to open the St Chad's underpass, 27th May 1968. Overseeing the operation is the Chairman of the Public Works Department, Alderman Shaw.

Duddeston Manor Road, 1968.

Old Cross Street, Gosta Green, May 1968.

Bordesley Green, between Palace Road and Charles Road, 14th June 1968.

Bristol Road South, with the traffic lights at the Bell Inn just out of sight on the left, Northfield, June 1968.

Coventry Road, with St Oswald's Road just round to the right, Small Heath, 25th June 1968.

Corporation Street, 1968.

The Lady Mayoress, Mrs Charles Simpson, attends a World Children's Day service and meets some of the children, along with the Provost of Birmingham, the Rt Rev George Sinker, St Philips, 14th June 1968.

Tony Hancock, Birmingham's favourite comic, is found dead in Australia, 25th June 1968. Here, in happier days, he arrives to entertain at the RAF station, at Nicosia, in Cyprus.

Members of the City of Birmingham Symphony Orchestra set out on their Easter European tour, 28th June 1968.

Hingeston Street/Ellen Street, Hockley, 12th July 1968.

Alcester Road, not far from Chantry Road, on the left, Moseley, 1968.

Office staff, Cadbury Bros Ltd., Bournville, Summer 1968.

Dudley Road, with Western Road ahead, Spring Hill, 30th July 1968.

Lower Loveday Street, 3rd October 1968.

The new bridge, over the River Tame, opens after damage by flood water, Great Barr, 14th October 1968.
It was part of the commuter line between Walsall and the city.

Comedian, Norman Wisdom, meets Violet Ensor,
relief manageress at the ABC cinema, Aston, on her
70th birthday, 19th October 1968.

Ladypool Road, with Highgate Road at the traffic lights,
Sparkbrook, November 1968.

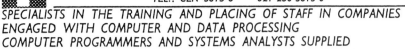

The Queen Mother, as gracious as ever, leaves after attending the consecration of the new St Peter's Church, by the Bishop of Birmingham, Dr John Wilson, Tile Cross, 13th November 1968.

Colmore Row, 19th January 1969.

As demolition goes on all around them, the Finnegan family wait to be re-housed, William Edward Street, Highgate, 11th March 1969.

St Vincent Street/King Edward's Road, 23rd April 1969. Note the ornate Victorian loo, just one of many dotted around the city at the time.

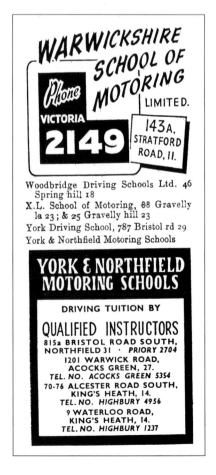

Members of Aston Villa FC and Delta Metal FC combine to make a happy picture, Villa Park, 1969. The ensuing match was a "thank you" to Delta for allowing the Villa to use their ground for training purposes.

The Red Devil motor cyclists are greeted by the Lord Mayor, Alderman Neville Bosworth,
Council House, 21st May 1969.

Meanwhile, the Lady Mayoress, Mrs Marion Bosworth, opens the Greaves Hall Play Group Tufty Club,
Kings Norton, 21st May 1969. Tufty was a stuffed squirrel used to promote road safety.

SUBURBIA was shaken in June when plans for the massive local government shake-up were announced.

Birmingham's "upper crust" neighbours, Sutton Coldfield and Solihull, were shocked to learn that they were both to be absorbed by the city.

In the event, only Sutton was landed with a Birmingham address. Solihull remained independent but enlarged — taking in Chelmsley Wood among others.

THE WORLD watched and held its breath as millions of television sets received the hazy picture of astronaut Neil Armstrong reaching the bottom rung of the ladder leading down from the spacecraft Eagle.

The now legendary words rang out across space as his feet gingerly tested the lunar dust: "That was one small step for man, but one giant leap for mankind."

The date was July 21, 1969. Man was on the moon.

Neil Armstrong, whose exploits excited the whole world. Not many people realised that he was actually a civilian employee at NASA who had been designated a flight commander.

St Peter's Place and St Martin's Place, off Broad Street, 18th July 1969.

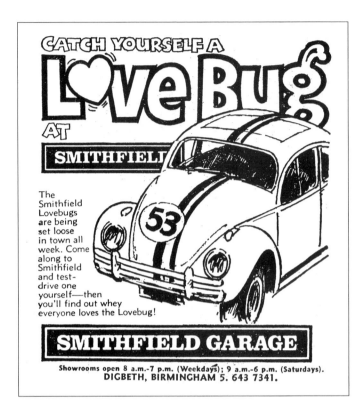
Heathfield Road, Handsworth, 21st August 1969.

Harold Gray brings the CBSO and the audience to its feet at the last night of the Proms, Town Hall,
30th August 1969.

Landor Street, Saltley, 1969.

Work on the Gravelly Hill interchange, from Copeley Hill, 6th October 1969.

Clifton Road, Aston, 1969. Upper Sutton Street would have been just to the left of Mrs Priest's drapery shop.

Smallbrook Ringway, October 1969.

Disc jockey and singer, Jimmy Young, besieged by members of the public, Evening Mail Stand,
Ideal Home Exhibition, Bingley Hall, 17th October 1969. He was there to promote Bio-Strath, a herbal
yeast tonic – quite appropriate for someone who went on to reinvent himself and take on a new life as
one of our foremost radio personalities.

Sheaf Lane, just before you reach Coventry Road on the right, Sheldon, 19th November 1969.

Hagley Road, with Wyndham Road on the left, 27th November 1969.

Main production line, Eddystone Radio Ltd., Alvechurch Road, West Heath,
December 1969.

Birmingham is now almost certain
to be chosen as the site for the new
national exhibition centre.

It is understood that an option has been
placed on one of two sites near Birmingham
Airport, at Elmdon, where it is planned to
build a £10 million exhibition complex.

This became known last night after Mr. Roy
Mason, President of the Board of Trade, had made
a statement in the House of Commons, saying that
the only proposal receiving very urgent considera-
tion was for the centre at Birmingham.